MY FAMILY & ME

An Inclusive Family Tree Activity Book

Sam Hutchinson • Illustrated by Vicky Barker

Contents

FOR
YOUNG
READERS

This book belongs to:

Racehorse for Young Readers books may be purchased in bulk at special discounts for sales promotions, corporate gifts, fund-raising or education purposes. Special editions can also be created to specifications. For details, contact the Special Sales Department at Skyhorse Publishing, 307 West 36th Street, 11th Floor, New York, NY 10018 or info@skyhorsepublishing.com. Racehorse for Young Readers is a pending trademark of Skyhorse Publishing, Inc.®, a Delaware corporation.

Visit our website at skyhorsepublishing.com

10 9 8 7 6 5 4 3 2 1

Art director: Vicky Barker
Additional design: Kim Hankinson Publisher: Sam Hutchinson
Co-authors of original editions: Lone Morton, Catherine Bruzzone & Tat Small

With thanks to Beth and Alex at Inclusive Minds for their inclusivity and diversity consultancy.

Print ISBN: 978-1-63158-661-3

Printed in China

ALL ABOUT ME

More about me

The following pages are for you to fill in with details about yourself, your friends, where you learn, and things you like doing. Later, you will also fill in details of your family and the people who look after you. You may collect more information, photos, or souvenirs than you have room for on these pages, so here are some ideas for keeping everything together:

You can clip extra paper to the pages, like this:

Or you can make a special pocket on the inside of the back cover, like this:

Cut a triangle from card. Glue or tape it to the bottom right of a page or inside the front cover.

Or you can make a separate book, like this:

To keep your book and extra paper together, tie a ribbon round them, like this:

Punch holes in the extra paper. Thread through pieces of wool to hold them together.

This will be a wonderful record to read again and again as you get older. If you have children of your own, you can even show it to them!

Self-portrait

Look in the mirror to help you draw a picture of yourself here.

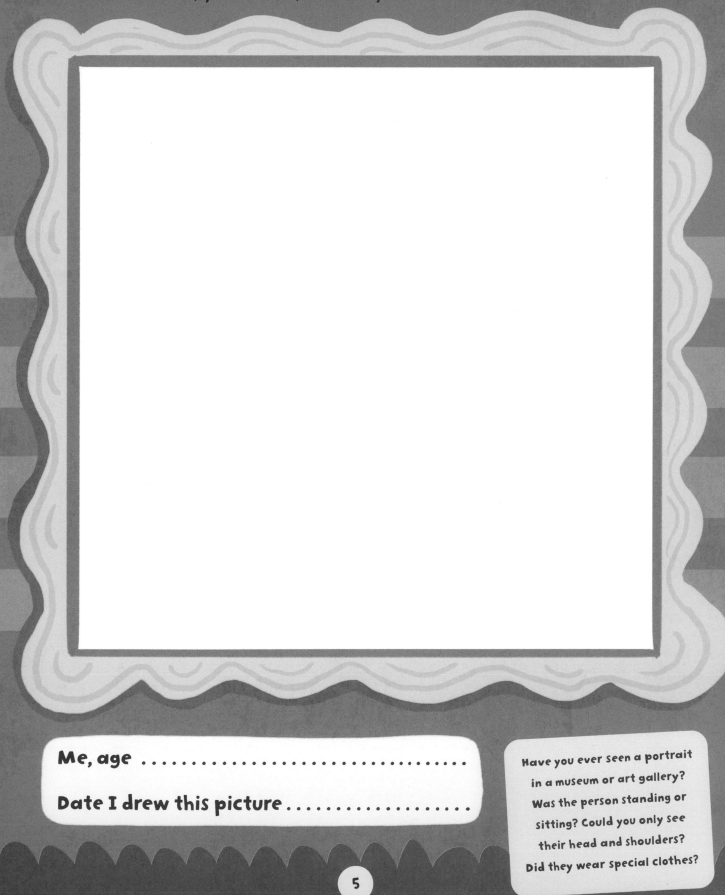

Me, age . . . .

Date I drew this picture . . . .

Have you ever seen a portrait in a museum or art gallery? Was the person standing or sitting? Could you only see their head and shoulders? Did they wear special clothes?

Me

My name is
....

My birthday

Where I was born

....

Year I was born

My earliest recorded weight

....

Day of the week I was born

My earliest recorded height

....

Stick in a photo

The earliest photo of me

Nationality

Languages I can speak

....

....

Color of eyes

....

Color of hair

....

My thumbprint

Practice this on a separate piece of paper before you start. Paint your thumb with a bright color. Let it dry slightly. Then press it firmly on the paper and roll it carefully from side to side without lifting it up.

This is a lock of my hair

Ask an adult to help you cut a small lock of hair.

Age I am now

Today's date

....

Height I am now

....

My hand span

....

Why not make a handprint and a footprint too? Do them on separate sheets of paper and clip them to this page or start an extra book. Look at the suggestions for this on page 4.

Stick in a photo

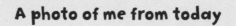

A photo of me from today

What time I woke up today

....

What I wore today

....

Where I went today

....

....

What I ate today

....

The best part of today

....

The worst part of today

....

Musical instruments I like

· ·

· ·

Activities I want to do

· ·

· ·

· ·

Don't forget any activities you do at the weekend.

Sports I like

I like...

riding a bike

swimming

reading

working on the computer

cleaning my room

drawing

being outdoors

List any other things you can do.

I can...

· ·

· ·

· ·

What makes me happy

··

··

Something that's important to me

··

··

What makes me sad

··

··

Something amazing I have learned

··

··

My worst habit

··

··

Something I'm really good at

··

··

My signature

Something I'm really good at

The best thing about me

··

··

Who I live with

Draw a picture of someone you live with. If you live with lots of people and need more space then use an extra piece of paper.

Name and age

1.
....

Best thing about them

....

What we do together

....

Name and age

2.
....

Best thing about them

....

What we do together

....

Name and age

3.
....

Best thing about them

....

What we do together

....

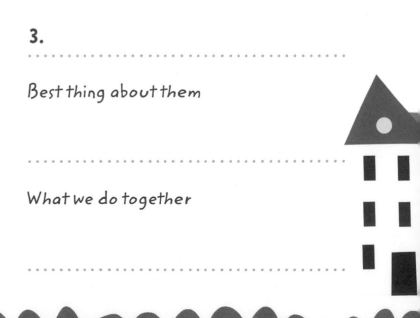

Names of other important people in your life—or pets!

....

....

....

Stick in a photo of important people in your life

Write the names of the people in the photo. When was it taken?

....

....

Different people in my life

Write the names of all the important people in your life at the end of the lines. You could write in a different color if they're members of your family. Do you know the name of any of their relations? If so, add more lines on a separate piece of paper and write their names, too.

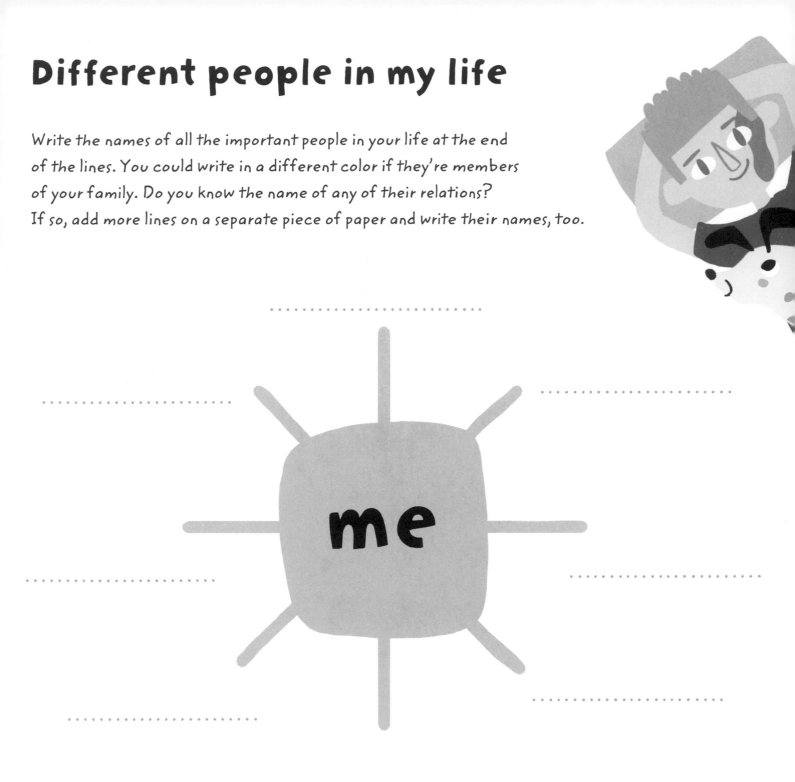

Families come in all shapes and sizes. Your family is unique. When filling this in, include details of any step family, half-sisters or brothers, aunts, uncles, and cousins. Some people have large families and might need extra sheets of paper. Add information about any other people in your family here or on an extra piece of paper. Your family, your rules!

Where I live

My address

My telephone number

....

....

....

Email

....

....

If you draw a block of apartments or a street, put an arrow to mark where you live.

This is where I live

Can you find an old postcard or photo showing your neighborhood in the past? Can you ask your older relatives or neighbors about it?

The neighborhood where I live is

. . . .

Describe the area where you live. Is it a big city or a small town? Is it a village or the middle of the country? Is it in the mountains or near the sea?

Map of my neighborhood

You may need help with this. You can mark your home, your nearest shop, your school, the nearest bus stop or railway station.

Names of my nearest neighbors

. . . .

. . . .

. . . .

. . . .

The most special thing about where I live is

. . . .

. . . .

The worst thing about where I live is

. . . .

. . . .

My bedroom

Color of my walls

....

Color of my curtains or blinds

....

Posters or pictures I have on my wall

....

View from my window

....

Best thing about my room

....

Worst thing about my room

....

Draw your own bed with your favorite duvet cover and toys.

My school

If you learn at home, then write about that on these pages.

Do you learn at school or at home?

....

Stick in a photo

Where I learn

Address

....

....

Telephone number

Name of the person in charge

....

Name of the person who teaches me

....

....

Draw the person who teaches you here.

Name or number of my class

....

Number of children where I learn

Names of the friends I learn with

....

....

....

Kids I like to sit next to

....

....

....

....

I start school at .... o'clock

I finish school at .... o'clock

start   finish

My favorite lesson

....

My least favorite lesson

....

Clubs

....

....

This is a typical week at school (or home). Fill it in, including the days of the week.

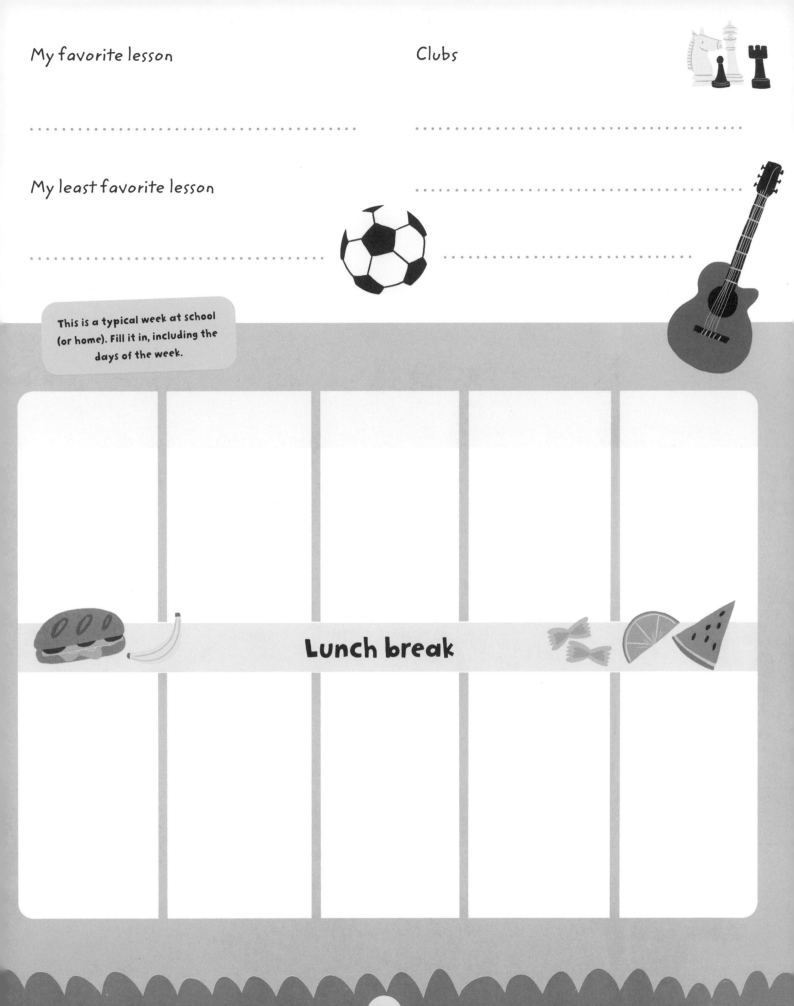

Lunch break

My favorite lunch

If you have a packed lunch, you can still draw it on the plate.

My favorite school outing

....

....

....

....

....

My favorite school joke

....

....

What I do at break time

....

....

....

....

Do you know any skipping games or playground rhymes? Write them on a piece of paper and clip them to this page.

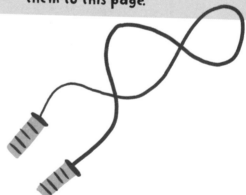

Draw a picture or stick in a postcard or a souvenir such as a bus ticket or a museum ticket.

My friends

Draw yourself and one of your best friends here.

One of my best friends is

....

Their birthday

....

Why are you such good friends?

....

....

....

....

Some of my other friends are:

1.

....

How we met and why we are friends

....

....

....

....

2.

....

How we met and why we are friends

....

....

....

....

Write a poem about a friend—it could be a real friend or an imaginary friend.

Something nice I've done for my friend

Something nice my friend has done for me

Draw what you and your friends enjoy doing together.

Design badges for your friends and family.

To make these badges, trace these templates on to cardstock and cut them out. Tape a safety pin on the back. Be careful with the pin!

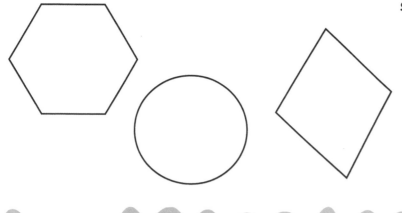

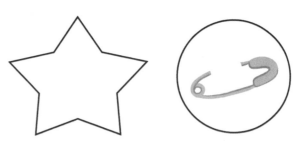

My likes and dislikes

My favorite color

....

My favorite TV program

....

My favorite book or author

....

My favorite sport

....

My least favorite color

....

My least favorite TV program

....

A book I didn't enjoy

....

My least favorite sport

....

My likes and dislikes

This is my favorite food.

This is the food I dislike.

My favorite film

....

A film which scared me

....

A cartoon character I want to be like

....

My favorite song

....

My favorite time of year

....

What I want to do before my next birthday

....

....

The best day of my life was

....

....

....

The worst day of my life was

....

....

What I enjoy doing most in the world

....

....

My clothes

What I like wearing best

....

What I dislike wearing

....

What I wear at night

....

What I wear to school

....

The color of my shoes

....

My dream fancy dress outfit

....

Design a T-shirt.

Next draw your dream outfit on an extra sheet of blank paper. Stick on little samples of material. Color and label your costume.

Pets and animals

My favorite animal

....

The pet I own or would like to have

....

My pet's name

....

My pet's age

....

What my pet eats

....

Where my pet sleeps

....

The best thing about my pet

....

....

....

If you don't have a pet, write about your favorite animal or a pet you would like to own.

Stick in a photo or drawing

My pet or favorite animal

Does your type of pet also live in the wild? Which country does it come from? Is it a hot or cold country? Find that country on this map.

The country where I live

Name of my country

This is my
country's flag

....

Capital city

Highest mountain

....

Main language or languages spoken

Longest river

....

Map of the country where I live

Mark where you
live on the map.

My holidays

Time I get up during the holidays

....

Time I go to bed

....

My favorite holiday activity

....

What I don't like about holidays

....

What I did on my last holiday

....

What I'd like to do on my next holiday

....

Collect a souvenir from a place you visited in the holidays such as a postcard, stamp, or a candy wrapper.

Design a stamp for your postcard!

Write a postcard to a friend from your dream vacation. Or draw a picture.

Me in the future

My age on my next birthday

....

What I want to do on my next birthday

....

My next school

....

Something new I want to try

....

Something I want to stop doing

....

What I want to do when I grow up

....

....

Design some badges for yourself. Look back at page 24 to see how to make them.

I can READ!

I ♥ swimming

I want to be an astronaut

I'm brilliant!

A wish for the future

32

MY FAMILY TREE

What is a family tree?

Your family tree is the map of your family. It shows how you are related, or joined, to the other people in **your** family—just like the branches and twigs are joined to the trunk of a tree.

The picture opposite shows an example of a family tree. Can you see the lines joining the sister, parents, and grandparents? These lines show how they are **related**. These people are **relatives**.

This may not look like your family. Perhaps you have more or fewer brothers or sisters? You may have aunts and uncles and lots of cousins. You may think of some of your friends as your family. Family trees can show all these people. They can also give you fascinating facts, like when your parent or parents were born, how many brothers and sisters a grandparent has, or how old a great grandparent was when they passed away. Families are all different.

You will be able to draw your own family tree at the end of this book. Families come in all shapes and sizes and we show some exciting and different trees later on pages 52 to 59. But before you do, discover as much as you can about your family on the next pages. You may already have written in some general information on pages 11 to 13. Now you can include more details. You won't fill in all the spaces—or you might need extra pages for even more answers. **Your family, your rules!**

If you need more space, look back at page 4 for how to add extra information to the book.

This is an example of one type of family tree. Remember, every family is different, so you will probably leave some bits blank when you make your own family tree.

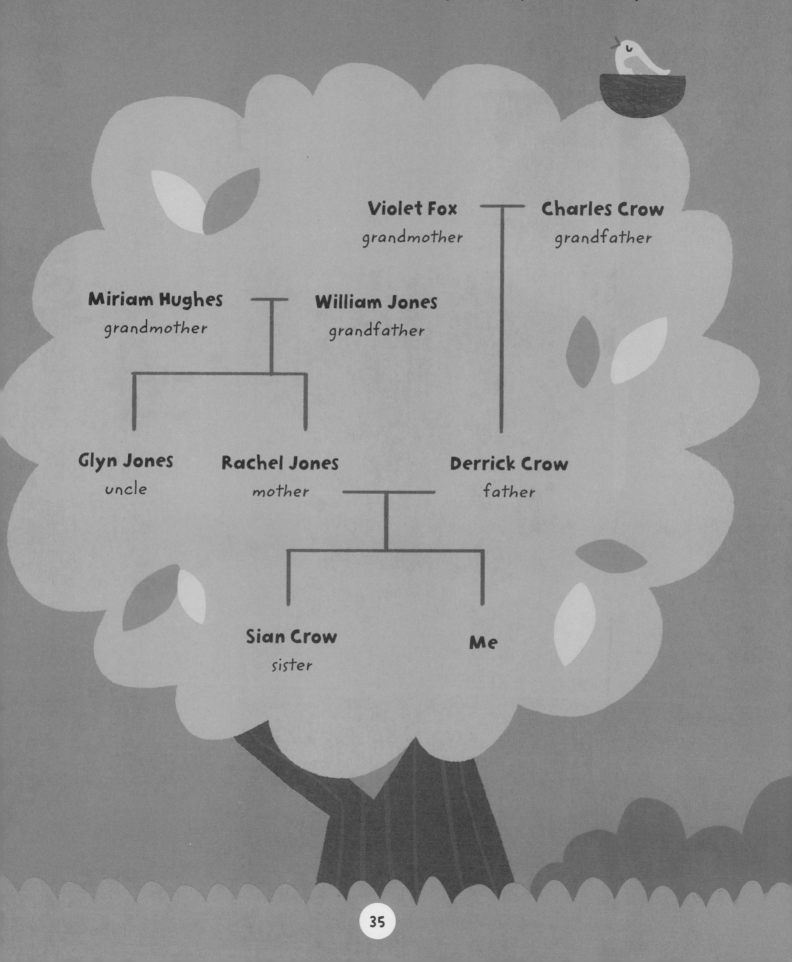

Violet Fox
grandmother

Charles Crow
grandfather

Miriam Hughes
grandmother

William Jones
grandfather

Glyn Jones
uncle

Rachel Jones
mother

Derrick Crow
father

Sian Crow
sister

Me

Moms and dads

On pages 5 to 7, you filled in important information about yourself. These next four pages are where you can collect information about your parent or parents. Every family is different, so use these four pages to discover your family. Take extra sheets of paper if you need them and clip them into the book. And remember, you won't be filling in all the information. This is your family. Start by writing about one parent.

I call them

....

Their birthday

....

Year they were born

....

Where they were born

....

They have .... brothers

They have .... sisters

Names of any brothers

....

Names of any sisters

....

Names of schools they went to

....

My ...., age ...

My ...., age ...

Their full name is ....

A memory from their school days   Favorite color

....

....   Favorite food

Can you find their high school or college degrees? Did they do gymnastics, science activities, or chess club?

Jobs

....

Their age when I was born

....

Color of their hair

....

Color of their eyes

....

Draw your parent here.

My parent

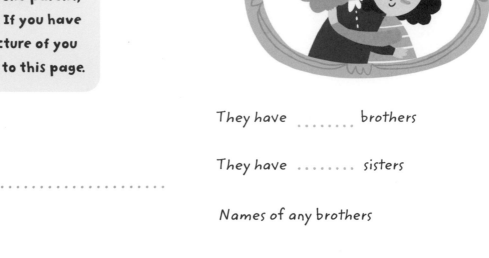

If you have more than one parent, write about them here. If you have one parent, draw a picture of you together and attach it to this page.

I call them

. . . .

Their birthday

. . . .

Year they were born

. . . .

Where they were born

. . . .

They have . . . . brothers

They have . . . . sisters

Names of any brothers

. . . .

Names of any sisters

. . . .

Names of schools they went to

. . . .

Stick in a photo

My . . . . , age . . .

Stick in a photo

My . . . . , age . . .

Their full name is ....

A memory from their school days

....

....

Can you find their high school or college degrees? Did they do gymnastics, science activities, or chess club?

Jobs

....

Their age when I was born

....

Color of their hair

....

Color of their eyes

....

Favorite color

....

Favorite food

....

Draw your parent here.

My sisters and brothers

If you don't have any brothers or sisters, put "0" in the boxes below. Stick a drawing of your family over this page. Or write about an imaginary brother or sister.

Number of sisters .... Number of brothers ....

My oldest sister or brother is named

....

Date they were born

....

Where they were born

....

My next oldest sister or brother is named

....

Date they were born

....

Where they were born

....

My next oldest sister or brother is named

....

Date they were born

....

Where they were born

....

If you have more than three sisters and brothers, write their details on a piece of paper and clip it to this page. Some of your sisters or brothers might be step- or half-sisters or brothers. If you want to, you can write more details about them or how you are related to them: "Rose is my half-sister. She and I have the same father." "Robert is my step-brother. He is John's son. John lives with my mother."

Stick in
a photo

My . . . . , age . . . .

Stick in
a photo

My . . . . , age . . . .

Who is in each photo?
How old are they?
Where were the
photos taken? When
were they taken?

. . . .

. . . .

. . . .

My aunts and uncles

Aunts and uncles are your parents' sisters and brothers.
If your parent doesn't have any sisters or brothers, write
about other adults who spend a lot of time with your family.
Some families call close friends "uncle" or "aunt."

Related to, or friends with my

....

Name

Name

....

Date they were born

Date they were born

....

Where they were born

Where they were born

....

Where they live now

Where they live now

....

Names of children

Names of children

....

Your aunts' or uncles' children
are your cousins. You can fill
in more detail about them on
pages 46 and 47.

Name

....

Date they were born

....

Where they were born

....

Where they live now

....

Names of children

....

Stick in a photo

If your parent has more than three sisters and brothers, write their details on a piece of paper and clip it here. Can you find a photo of them all together as kids?

Stick in a photo

....

Write the names of the people in each photo. Where were the photos taken? When were they taken? Do you have a photo of the same people now?

....

More of my aunts and uncles

Related to, or friends with my

....

Name	Name
....	....
Date they were born	Date they were born
....	....
Where they were born	Where they were born
....	....
Where they live now	Where they live now
....	....
Names of children	Names of children
....	....
....	....

Name

....

Date they were born

....

Where they were born

....

Where they live now

....

Names of children

....

If your parent has more than three sisters and brothers, write their details on a piece of paper and clip it here. Can you find a photo of them all together as children?

Stick in a photo

Stick in a photo

....

....

Write the names of the people in each photo. Where were the photos taken? When were they taken? Do you have a photo of the same people now?

My cousins

Some families use the word "cousin" for the children of your parents' sisters and brothers. Some families use the word "cousin" for other relatives as well or even very close family friends.

If your parent comes from a large family, you may have lots of cousins! First put their oldest brother or sister's name and then fill in the details for each cousin.

Name of oldest cousin

Name of next oldest cousin

Their parents' names

Their parents' names

Date and place they were born

Date and place they were born

What we do together

What we do together

More of my cousins

Paste a photo of your cousins on a sheet of paper. Under it, write their names and how old they are.

Name of oldest cousin

Name of next oldest cousin

....

Their parents' names

Their parents' names

....

Date and place they were born

Date and place they were born

....

What we do together

What we do together

....

....

If you don't have a photo of your cousins, draw a picture of them. Which of your cousins is the tallest and which is the smallest?

My grandparent

Grandparents are your parents' parents, or the people who raised your parents. If your grandparents are no longer alive, you may need to do some detective work to fill in these pages. Can your parents help?

Stick in a photo

My grandparent, age . . . .

The people on this page looked after my

....

Their name is

....

Name I call them

....

Date they were born

....

Where they were born

....

Name of school

....

Names of any sisters

....

Names of any brothers

....

Jobs

....

Their age when my mom or dad was born

....

Something they remember from the past

....

My grandparent

The people on this page looked after my

....

Their name is

....

Name I call them

....

Date they were born

....

Where they were born

....

Name of school

....

Names of any sisters

....

Names of any brothers

....

Jobs

....

Their age when my mom or dad was born

....

Something they remember from the past

....

....

Stick in a photo

My grandparent, age . . . .

Ask about the things that were different when your grandparents were young. What style of clothes did they wear? What games did they play? Can they remember something important in the news? Why not make a book or an audio recording of their memories?

My grandparent

If your grandparents are no longer alive, you may need to do some detective work to fill in these pages. Can your parents help? Or your aunts and uncles?

Stick in a photo

My grandparent, age . . . .

The people on this page looked after my

....

Their name is

....

Name I call them

....

Date they were born

....

Where they were born

....

Name of school

....

Names of any sisters

....

Names of any brothers

....

Jobs

....

Their age when my mom or dad was born

....

Something they remember from the past

....

My grandparent

The people on this page looked after my

....

Their name is

....

Name I call them

....

Date they were born

....

Where they were born

....

Name of school

....

Names of any sisters

....

Names of any brothers

....

Jobs

....

Their age when my mom or dad was born

....

Something they remember from the past

....

Do any of your grandparents have a marriage certificate? It will show you when and where they were married. If not, ask them about their first home.

Stick in a photo

My grandparent, age . . . .

Family groups

Many family tree designs look like actual trees with you at the bottom and your family making up the branches above.

Since all families are unique, you can sometimes make small trees with only a few branches. Or you might have huge trees with lots of branches. A big tree is very hard to draw and might not work for your family.

Start by putting the important people in your life into different "Family Groups." Look at the example on the opposite page.

Remember, this is your family and you might not be able to fill in every group.

Example groups

My parent or someone who looks after me

My parent

Foster family

Me

My step family

Birth family

Other important people

My own family tree

Fill in your own family tree here.

To start with, do a simple one—just any sisters or brothers, any parents and grandparents. For brothers and sisters, put the eldest on your left and the younger ones on your right. (Look at the tree on page 35 as a guide.)

If you want, ask someone to help you make a larger tree. This could show aunts and uncles, cousins and perhaps grandparents' brothers and sisters—or even great-grandparents! You could add more detail to your tree, like:

b. – born
m. – married
d. – died

Granny Hughes
b. 1 June 1949

Turn over and look at the following ideas for family trees if this design doesn't work for you.

See instructions for tracing on page 56. Cut out and color in faces for your tree from page 61.

Full family wheel

This family wheel might suit your family better than the tree on page 55.

Change the different sections of the wheel so that you can include all of the people in your family.

To create your own family wheel, place a piece of tracing paper over the template. Hold steady and draw around the shape. Turn the tracing paper over and scribble over the lines with a soft pencil. Turn over again and tape on to paper or cardstock. Retrace firmly over the original lines. Remove tracing paper.

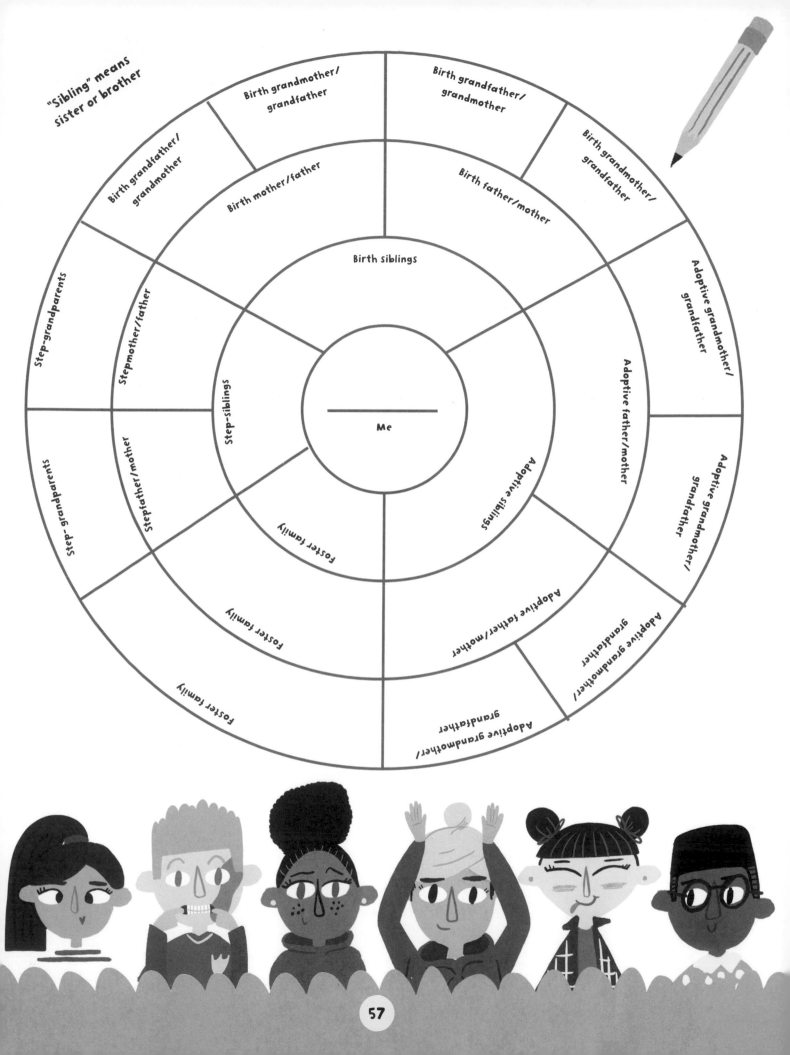

"Sibling" means sister or brother

Birth grandfather/grandmother
Birth grandmother/grandfather
Birth grandfather/grandmother
Birth grandmother/grandfather
Birth mother/father
Birth father/mother
Step-grandparents
Stepmother/father
Birth siblings
Adoptive grandmother/grandfather
Adoptive father/mother
Step-grandparents
Stepfather/mother
Step-siblings
Me
Adoptive father/mother
Adoptive grandmother/grandfather
Foster family
Adoptive siblings
Foster family
Adoptive father/mother
Adoptive grandmother/grandfather
Foster family
Adoptive grandmother/grandfather

Solo parent family tree

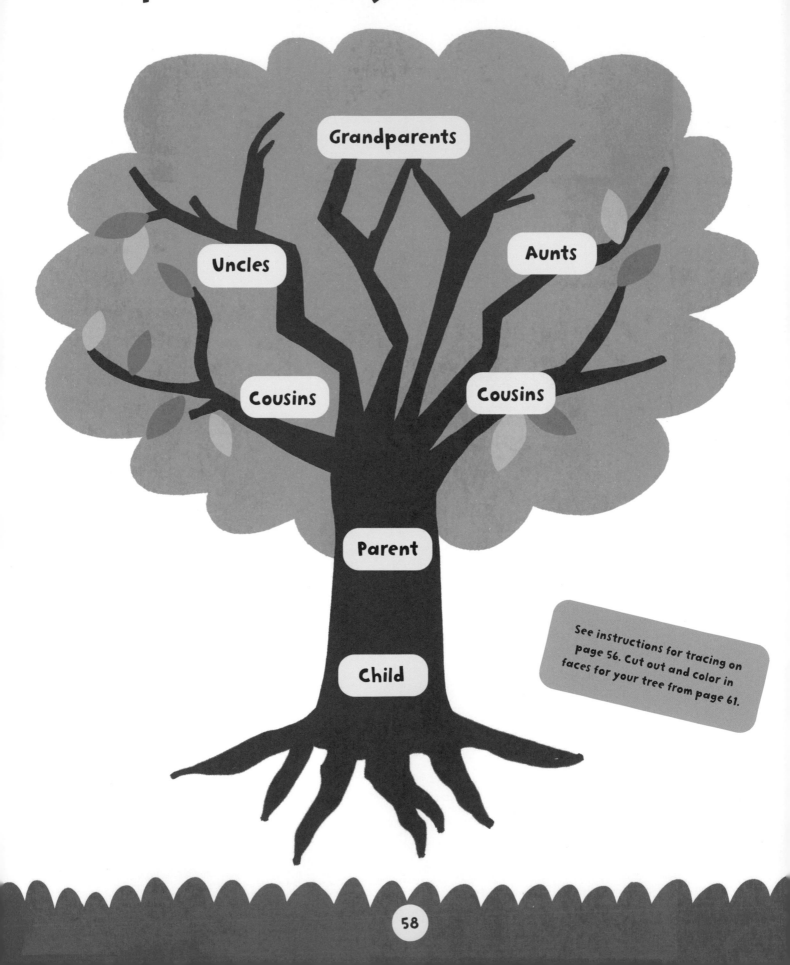

Grandparents

Uncles

Aunts

Cousins

Cousins

Parent

Child

See instructions for tracing on page 56. Cut out and color in faces for your tree from page 61.

Tree for adopted children

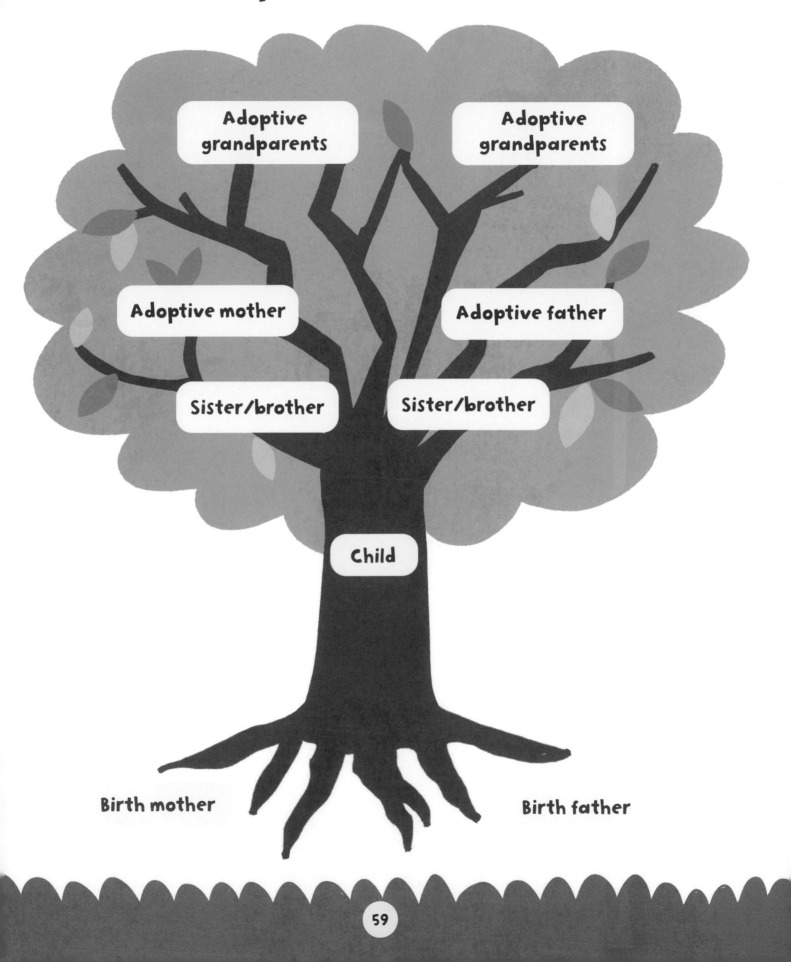

Adoptive grandparents

Adoptive grandparents

Adoptive mother

Adoptive father

Sister/brother

Sister/brother

Child

Birth mother

Birth father

Discovering more about your family

Did anyone in your family keep their school reports? They will be very interesting—and may be funny too!

In your local library, you can find out more about the year you were born and the years your family members were born. What style of clothes did people wear? What songs did they enjoy?

What new things were invented? Can your teacher help you?

Do any family members have any letters or papers to show how much they earned in their first jobs? Or perhaps old uniforms or pictures of themselves at work?

What about the place you or your family were born? Can you find old postcards of the past?

Did anyone in your family keep a diary? Perhaps of a special occasion or a family holiday?

Ask to see old tombstones, old samplers or old family books (like someone's copy of the Bible, Quran, Torah, or other books). These could help you discover even more about your family.

If some of your family come from another part of the world, trace or photocopy a map and mark the different countries.

Look up books about tracing your family tree in your local library, or search online.

Cut out and color in the members of your family tree.

61

Create a design to go on your door that tells people all about you.

Cut out the sign with the help
of an adult and stick it to your
bedroom door or a special place.